D1499723

My Favorite COLOR
YELLOW

A Crabtree Roots Book

AMY CULLIFORD

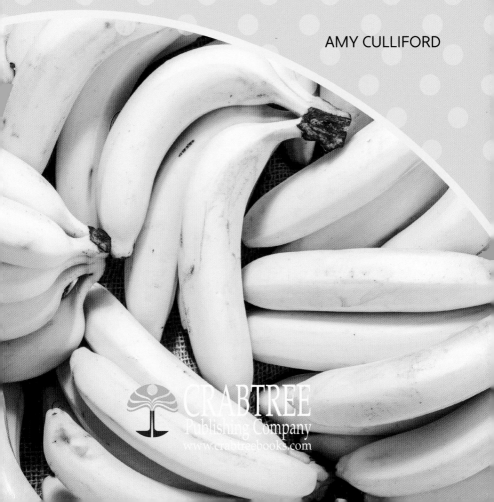

CRABTREE
Publishing Company
www.crabtreebooks.com

School-to-Home Support for Caregivers and Teachers

This book helps children grow by letting them practice reading. Here are a few guiding questions to help the reader with building his or her comprehension skills. Possible answers appear here in red.

Before Reading:
• What do I think this book is about?
- *This book is about the color yellow.*
- *This book is about things that are yellow.*

• What do I want to learn about this topic?
- *I want to learn what animals are yellow.*
- *I want to learn about shades of yellow.*

During Reading:
• I wonder why...
- *I wonder why the sun is yellow.*
- *I wonder why some buses are yellow.*

• What have I learned so far?
- *I have learned that chicks are yellow.*
- *I have learned that the sun is yellow.*

After Reading:
• What details did I learn about this topic?
- *I have learned that there are many shades of yellow.*
- *I have learned that flowers can be yellow.*

• Read the book again and look for the vocabulary words.
- *I see the word **bus** on page 6 and the word **chick** on page 8. The other vocabulary words are found on page 14.*

I see yellow.

I see the yellow **sun**.

I see a yellow **bus**.

I see a yellow **chick**.

I see a yellow **flower**.

What do you see
that is yellow?

Word List

Sight Words

a	is	what
do	see	yellow
I	the	you

Words to Know

bus

chick

flower

sun

I see yellow.

I see the yellow **sun**.

I see a yellow **bus**.

I see a yellow **chick**.

I see a yellow **flower**.

What do you see
that is yellow?

My Favorite **COLOR**

YELLOW

Written by: Amy Culliford

Designed by: Rhea Wallace

Series Development: James Earley

Proofreader: Kathy Middleton

Educational Consultant:
   Christina Lemke M.Ed.

Photographs:
Shutterstock: Valentina ProSkurina:
   cover; Hanna_photo: p. 1; Yellow Cat:
   p. 3; wemai: p. 4-5, 14; Elnur: p. 6-7,
   14; irin-k: p. 9, 14; Bhupinder Bagga:
   p. 11, 14; Evgeny Atamanenko: p. 13

Library and Archives Canada Cataloguing in Publication
Title: Yellow / Amy Culliford.
Names: Culliford, Amy, 1992- author.
Description: Series statement: My favorite color |
   "A Crabtree roots book".
Identifiers: Canadiana (print) 20200384031 |
   Canadiana (ebook) 2020038404X |
   ISBN 9781427134714 (hardcover) |
   ISBN 9781427132628 (softcover) |
   ISBN 9781427132680 (HTML)
Subjects: LCSH: Yellow—Juvenile literature.
Classification: LCC QC495.5 .C856 2021 | DDC j535.6—dc23

Library of Congress Cataloging-in-Publication Data
Title: Yellow / Amy Culliford.
Description: New York, NY : Crabtree Publishing Company, 2021. |
   Series: My favorite color; a crabtree roots book | Includes index
Identifiers: LCCN 2020050167 (print) |
   LCCN 2020050168 (ebook) |
   ISBN 9781427134714 (hardcover) |
   ISBN 9781427132628 (paperback) |
   ISBN 9781427132680 (ebook)
Subjects: LCSH: Yellow--Juvenile literature. | Colors--Juvenile literatu
Classification: LCC QC495.5 .C859 2021 (print) | LCC QC495.5 (eboo
   DDC 535.6--dc23
LC record available at https://lccn.loc.gov/2020050167
LC ebook record available at https://lccn.loc.gov/2020050168

Crabtree Publishing Company

www.crabtreebooks.com   1-800-387-7650

Printed in the U.S.A./022021/CG20201130

Published in the United States
Crabtree Publishing
347 Fifth Avenue, Suite 1402-145
New York, NY, 10016

Published in Canada
Crabtree Publishing
616 Welland Ave.
St. Catharines, Ontario L2M 5V6